Minibeasts In a Pond

Sarah Ridley

Smart Apple Media

Smart Apple Media
P.O. Box 3263, Mankato, Minnesota 56002

Printed in the United States

Published by arrangement with the Watts Publishing
Group Ltd, London.

Library of Congress Cataloging-in-Publication Data

Ridley, Sarah, 1963-
   Minibeasts in a pond / Sarah Ridley.
      p. cm. -- (Where to find minibeasts)
   Includes index.
   Summary: "Profiles many insects and invertebrates
found in ponds, discussing their eating habits, habitats,
and survival skills"--Provided by publisher.
   ISBN 978-1-59920-324-9 (hardcover)
 1. Pond animals--Juvenile literature. 2. Freshwater
insects--Juvenile literature. 3. Freshwater
invertebrates--Juvenile literature. I. Title.
   QL146.3.R53 2010
   592'.17636--dc22

                                          2008044908

Series editor: Sarah Peutrill
Art director: Jonathan Hair
Design: Jane Hawkins
Illustrations: John Alston

9 8 7 6 5 4 3 2 1

The measurements for the minibeasts in this book are typical sizes for the type of species shown in the photograph. However, species may vary a great deal in size.

Picture credits and species guide:
Front cover top: Boys looking into pond, Ron Sutherland/Garden Picture Library/Alamy. **Front cover below:** Small Red Damselfly (*Ceriagrion tenellum*), Michael Stenden/Shutterstock. **2:** Adult dragonfly (*Odonata*) emerging from nymph, Dr. Morley Read/Shutterstock. **3:** Mosquito (*Culex sp*) larvae, Stephen Dalton/NHPA. **6:** Lily pond, Josef Bosak/Shutterstock. **6cl:** Caddis fly (*Trichoptera*) larva, alle/Shutterstock. **6c:** Common Pond skater (*Gerris lacustris*), Lukas Hejtman/Shutterstock. **6cr:** Dragonfly (*Odonata*), Phillip Date/Shutterstock. **7b:** Pond skater (*Gerris lacustris*) with prey, Stephen Dalton/NHPA. **8t:** Dragonfly (*Odonata*) over water, Lane V Erikson/Shutterstock. **8b:** Dragonfly (*Odonata*) eyes, Andrejs Pidjass/Shutterstock. **9t:** Blue-tailed Damselfly (*Ischnura elegans*), Jenny Horne/Shutterstock. **9b:** Dragonfly (*Odonata*), Michel Jean Paller/Shutterstock. **10:** Common Pond skater (*Gerris lacustris*), Vasily Koval/Shutterstock. **11t:** Water Measurer (*Hydrometra stagnorum*) with prey, Stephen Dalton/NHPA. **11b:** Whirligig beetles (*Gyrinus marinus*), Stephen Dalton/NHPA. **12t:** Net, Johanna Goodyear/Shutterstock. **12ca:** Boxes, Scott Rothstein/Shutterstock. **12c:** Spoon, Travis Klein/Shutterstock. **12b:** Plastic glasses, Homestudio/Shutterstock. **13t:** Pond dipping, Geray Sweeney/Corbis. **13b:** Washing hands, Shutterstock. **14t:** Great Water Boatman (*Notonecta glauca*), François Gilson/Biosphoto/Still Pictures. **14b:** Great Water Boatman (*Notonecta glauca*), Gerry Cambridge/NHPA. **15t:** Great Diving Beetle (*Dytiscus marginalis*), A. Hartl/Still Pictures. **15b:** Water spider (*Argyroneta aquatica*), Stephen Dalton/NHPA. **16t:** Mosquito (*Culex sp.*), Olga Khoroshunova/Shutterstock. **16c:** Mosquito (*Culex sp.*) egg raft, Stephen Dalton/NHPA. **16b:** Mosquito (*Culex sp.*) larvae, Stephen Dalton/NHPA. **17t:** Mosquito (*Culex sp.*) pupae, Stephen Dalton/NHPA. **17c:** Mosquito adult (*Culex sp.*) emerging from pupa, George Bernard/NHPA. **17b:** Mosquito (*Culex sp.*) feeding, Doug Matthews/Shutterstock. **18:** Leech (*Trocheta subviridis*), Michael Rose/FLPA. **19t:** Water Scorpion (*Nepa rubra*) with prey, Silvestris Fotoservice/FLPA. **19b:** Caddis fly (*Trichoptera*) larva, Hecker/Sauer/Still Pictures. **20t:** Great Diving Beetle (*Dytiscus marginalis*) larva taking a mosquito larva, John Shaw/NHPA. **20b:** Aeshna dragonfly (*Aeshna sp.*) larva eating stickleback, Stephen Dalton/NHPA. **21t:** Large Red Damselfly nymph (*Pyrrhosoma nymphula*), Gerry Cambridge/NHPA. **21b:** Mayfly larva (*Ephemera sp.*), LUTRA/NHPA. **22:** Common snail (*Helix aspersa*), Pakhnyushcha/Shutterstock. **23:** Great Pond Snail (*Lymnaea stagnalis*) eggs, Foto Natura Stock/FLPA. **24t:** Dragonflies (*Odonata*) mating, Uli Hamacher/Istockphoto. **24b:** Dragonfly (*Odonata*) nymph, Stephen Inglis/Shutterstock. **25t:** Dragonfly (*Odonata*) nymph, Zaycev Alexei Vladimirovich/Shutterstock. **25b:** Adult dragonfly (*Odonata*) emerging from nymph, Dr Moreley Read/Shutterstock. **31:** Common snail (*Helix aspersa*), Pakhnyushcha/Shutterstock.

Contents

Words in **bold** are in the glossary on pages 28–29.

 Ponds can be dangerous since they are often deeper than they look. Always take an adult with you to visit a pond.

Swarming with Lif

Ponds are home to countless minibeasts. They are an amazing **habitat** to explore. Summer is the best time to visit ponds. Look out for darting dragonflies and other moving minibeasts.

Pond Zones

Different minibeasts live in different areas of a pond. Some fly over the surface, others live in the pond water, and many live right at the bottom.

What is a Minibeast?

Minibeast is the name given to thousands of small **animals**. Although many are **insects**, others are not. Minibeasts do not have **backbones**, so scientists call them **invertebrates**.

TOP TIP!

Look out for boxes like this because they will help you become a good minibeast spotter. Always be careful around water and only visit a pond with an adult.

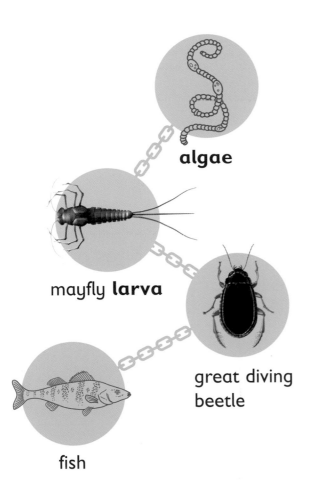

algae

mayfly **larva**

great diving beetle

fish

▶ A pond skater eats a fly that has fallen into the water.

A Pond Food Chain

While some pond minibeasts eat plants, most eat other minibeasts. Minibeasts themselves become meals for bigger pond animals, such as fish and toads. All these animals are linked in a **food chain**—from tiny plants and insects to big fish and birds.

Flying Over the Water

Look for dragonflies skimming over ponds. These flying insects have two pairs of wings and huge eyes.

▶ Dragonflies have lived around ponds and water since before the time of the dinosaurs—over 100 million years ago.

This dragonfly's **wingspan** is 2.4 inches (6 cm).

Fly Eats Fly

When dragonflies dart or hover over a pond, they are hunting for food. They catch their **prey** of midges and mosquitoes with their legs and then crunch them up in their powerful jaws.

◀ Dragonflies have huge eyes, called **compound eyes**, made up of thousands of tiny **lenses**. These help make them excellent hunters.

This damselfly is 1.6 inches (4 cm) long.

▲ There are several different types of damselfly. Some are red, others are blue or green.

Fluttery Damselflies

Damselflies are part of the dragonfly family but tend to be smaller and more delicate. They fly in a different way, too. Damselflies flutter like butterflies, instead of zooming in straight lines like dragonflies.

TOP TIP!

Sit on the bank of a pond—but not too close to the water. If you are lucky, a dragonfly (right) or damselfly will settle on the reeds. Watch how it rests. Damselflies fold their wings up while dragonflies hold them out to the sides.

Walking on Water

The pond skater, water measurer, and water beetle are **bugs** that can walk on water. These minibeasts hunt for food across the surface of a pond.

This pond skater's body is ⅜ inch (1 cm) long.

▲ A pond skater's legs are covered in hairs that trap air, which help prevent the bug from sinking.

The Pond Skater

The pond skater moves quickly across the surface of a pond and never gets wet. This is because it is very light and it spreads its weight across its six legs. It eats insects that have fallen into the pond. In turn, the pond skater is eaten by **predators** such as dragonflies and spiders.

The Slow Mover

The water measurer stays afloat in the same way as the pond skater, but it moves more slowly. It does not need to move fast because most of the insects it eats have fallen into the pond and cannot escape.

▼ The water measurer sucks its victim's body up through its mouth parts.

This water measurer is ⅜ inch (1 cm) long.

TOP TIP!

You are more likely to find a water measurer around the edge of the pond, or among pond plants.

These water beetles are ⁵⁄₁₆ inch (0.8 cm) long.

Busy Beetle

If you see small, shiny beetles zooming on the pond surface searching for food, they are probably water beetles. Unlike the other bugs on this page, they can dive under water to chase tiny insects.

◀ Water beetles live in groups of up to 60 beetles.

11

Pond Dipping

An excellent way to discover pond minibeasts is to go pond dipping.

 Always be careful near water! Take an adult with you.

You will need:
- A strong net with a long handle
- 3 plastic trays
- Plastic spoons or plastic cups
- A magnifying glass

What to do:
- Ask an adult to half fill your plastic collecting trays with pond water. Quickly sweep the net across the surface of the pond and then lower it into the first plastic tray. Turn the net inside out to release the contents. Lift out the net. What have you found?

- Now repeat the steps above but sweep the net under the water and empty the contents into a different plastic tray. Finally, let the net sink to the bottom of the pond and empty the net into a third plastic tray.

▲ You will need to half fill your plastic trays before you start pond dipping.

• Use a plastic spoon or cup to capture a minibeast for a closer look. A magnifying glass can give a new view of a really small creature. Use the identification guide on pages 26–27 to help you name the minibeasts.

• Be careful with minibeasts because it is easy to hurt them. Remember to return them all to the pond when you have finished.

⚠ Wash your hands after you have been pond dipping and before you eat!

Diving Down

Water boatmen and diving beetles swim down from the pond surface to hunt underwater minibeasts.

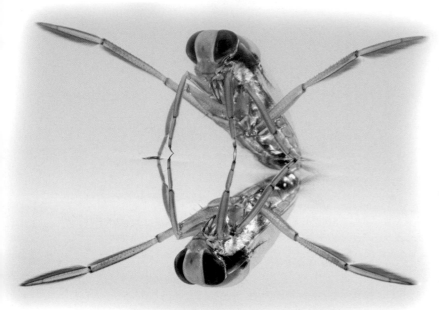

This water boatman is ¾ inch (2 cm) long.

Fast Swimmer

The water boatman actually swims upside down. Its back legs act like oars to power it through the water. It is a fierce hunter that will even tackle small fish and **tadpoles**, as well as insects.

◀ This water boatman is reflected in the surface of the water.

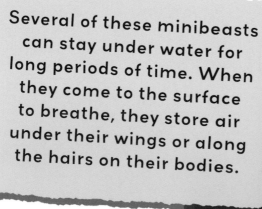

Several of these minibeasts can stay under water for long periods of time. When they come to the surface to breathe, they store air under their wings or along the hairs on their bodies.

▶ Trapped air bubbles make the water boatman look silver.

Fearsome Hunter

The great diving beetle is one of the largest pond minibeasts. Its big appetite means it will eat whatever it can catch. If food runs short, the beetle will fly to another pond at night.

▶ An adult great diving beetle can catch small fish.

This great diving beetle is 1.6 inches (4 cm) long.

This water spider is ⅜ inch (1 cm) long.

Water Spiders

Water spiders can live above the pond's surface but choose to spend most of their time under water. They spin a web attached to underwater pond plants and fill it with air that they bring down from the pond's surface.

Mosquito Life Cycle

In the summer, you may see small wriggling minibeasts. They are the young, the larvae, of mosquitoes.

This egg raft is 3⁄16 inch (5 mm) long.

1. Laying Eggs

Mosquitoes lay their eggs in floating "rafts" on the pond.

2. Growing Larvae

After a few days, the larvae hatch out. They hang with their tail ends at the surface to breathe. Their big mouths grab tiny bits of plants or animals from under the water.

③

Pupa

Empty larva skin

3. Pupae

As the larvae grow, they shed their skin and in just a few days they turn into **pupae**. At this stage they do not eat, but they can swim.

④

This mosquito is ⅜ inch (1 cm) long.

4. Adult

After a couple of days, the pupa splits open and the adult mosquito climbs out of the water and into the air.

▶ Mosquitoes feed on the blood of humans and other animals. They are not the most popular of minibeasts!

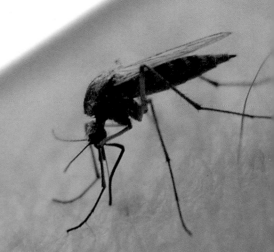

At the Bottom

At the bottom of the pond live minibeasts that you will rarely see. Living underneath the pond are leeches, water scorpions, and insect larvae.

This leech is 3.1 inches (8 cm) long.

▲ A leech rests among pond stones and plants.

Down in the Mud

Leeches rest in pond mud and grip onto stones or leaves. They attach themselves to a passing fish, tadpole, or larva and suck the blood from it. When they are full up, they let go and may not feed again for another month.

Water Scorpion

Crawling along the bottom of the pond, the water scorpion searches for minibeasts or tadpoles to grab with its front legs. It sucks out the insides with its sharp mouth.

◀ A water scorpion's long tail is its breathing tube. When it needs more air, it swims to the surface and hangs upside down to fill up with air again.

This water scorpion is ¾ inch (2 cm) long.

A Moving Twig

When you are pond dipping, you may find something that looks like a twig. If the "twig" moves, look more closely. This is a caddis fly larva, which has made an amazing home of leaves, stones and sand all stuck onto a tube of silk that it spun itself.

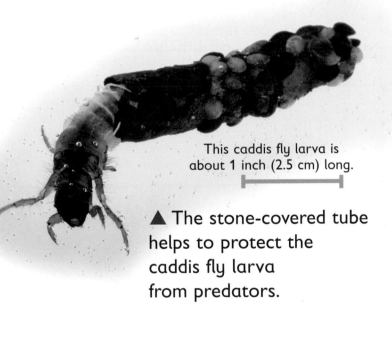

This caddis fly larva is about 1 inch (2.5 cm) long.

▲ The stone-covered tube helps to protect the caddis fly larva from predators.

▶ Not all caddis fly larvae cover themselves with stones and leaves.

Larvae and Nymphs

You are unlikely to see any of the animals on this page unless you go pond dipping. Along with the caddis fly larvae (page 19), these larvae and **nymphs** are underwater minibeasts.

This great diving beetle larva is 2 inches (5 cm) long.

Dangling Larva

The larva of the great diving beetle has a big appetite. It catches its prey while dangling from the surface upside down. It breathes through a tube in its tail.

▲ The great diving beetle larva pierces prey and sucks it up.

This dragonfly nymph is 1.6 inches (4 cm) long.

▲ The dragonfly nymph eats anything in the pond that is smaller than itself.

Dragonfly Nymph

The dragonfly nymph crawls around the bottom of the pond and uses its huge eyes to find food. It can breathe in water like a fish.

Damselfly Nymph

The damselfly nymph looks similar to the dragonfly nymph. However, it has three things that look like feathers on its tail. These allow it to breathe under water.

This damselfly nymph is 1.2 inches (3 cm) long.

Mayfly Nymph

If your pond dipping brings up a smaller-sized larva, it might be a mayfly nymph.

◀ The mayfly nymph eats tiny plants.

This mayfly nymph is ¾ inch (2 cm) long.

TOP TIP!

To decide which larvae you have found, look at the tail end:

dragonfly larva—short tail pieces
damselfly larva—longer, feather-like tail pieces
mayfly larva—long, slim tail pieces.

Snails at the Edge

Look at the plants growing near the edge of a pond and you may see pond snails.

Eating and Breathing

Pond snails eat algae, which are tiny plants that coat rocks or other water plants.

Some pond snails need to come to the surface to take on a fresh supply of air, while others can breathe in water.

◀ The pond snail's shell helps to protect its soft body.

This pond snail's shell is 2 inches (5 cm) long.

In winter, many pond snails bury themselves in the mud at the bottom of a pond. They seal themselves inside their shell and stay there until warmer weather returns in spring.

◀ Look out for spotted strips of jelly, often attached to pond plants. These are pond snail eggs covered in protective jelly. When the eggs hatch, tiny snails emerge.

How Snails Move

The snail glides along on its muscular "foot." The muscles in the foot get bigger and smaller, creating ripples of movement that push the snail forwards.

TOP TIP!

If you find a pond snail, you could keep it in a glass jar filled with pond water for a short while. Ask an adult to poke holes in the lid. Then you could watch the snail move up the glass jar.

Dragonfly Life Cycle

During its **life cycle**, the dragonfly lives in all areas of the pond.

1

1. Laying Eggs

Adult dragonflies skim above the pond, feeding on flies and other minibeasts. The females mate with males and lay eggs. Some dragonflies make slits in a plant stem and poke an egg inside, while others lay lots of eggs directly into the pond.

◀ Dragonflies make a circle shape when they mate.

2. Nymphs

2

When an egg hatches, out comes a nymph— a crawling, eating machine. It lives at the bottom of the pond for several months or even years, growing bigger and bigger, shedding its outer skin when it becomes too tight.

3. Coming Out of the Water

Each change of skin makes the nymph look more like an underwater dragonfly. Then one day it is time to change. The nymph climbs up a plant stem into the air.

▲ This nymph has the beginnings of wings.

4. Adult

The nymph's skin splits for the last time and out comes an adult dragonfly.

The dragonfly's life cycle from egg to the death of the adult varies. Some types have life cycles as short as six months, while others take six or seven years to reach adulthood.

▶ The adult leaves the pale ghost of its nymph skin attached to a plant stem.

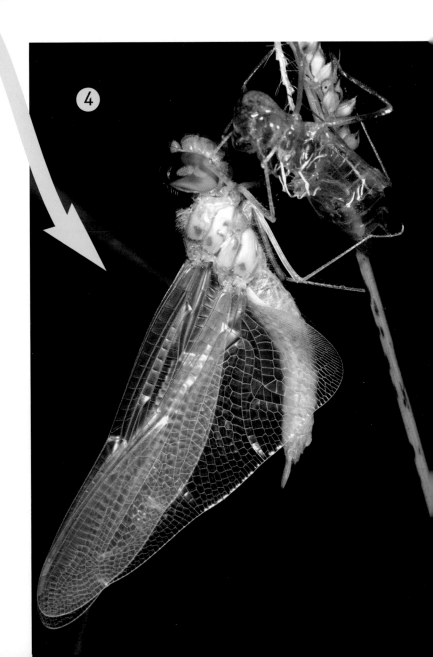

4

Identification Guide

In order of main appearance in this book:

Dragonfly: A flying insect, very similar to the damselfly. It usually rests with its wings held out from its body while the damselfly usually folds its wings above its body.

Water boatman: This insect belongs to the bug family and feeds on other minibeasts. It swims upside down using its long back legs as oars.

Damselfly: This flying insect has two pairs of wings and huge eyes. Like the dragonfly, it flies above the water catching small insects to eat.

Great diving beetle: A large, shiny water beetle that dives down to catch its prey. It uses its legs to swim through the water.

Midge: A tiny fly that often gathers in groups over the surface of a pond.

Water spider: All spiders have eight legs and a body in two parts. The water spider spins a silk "bubble" under the water to store air.

Pond skater: This pond insect can walk on water.

Mosquito: A blood-sucking fly that lays its eggs in water.

Water measurer: This long, slim insect spreads its weight on its long legs and slowly walks across water. It is a bug and feeds on other minibeasts.

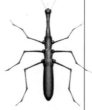

Mosquito larva: Small wriggling larva that hangs upside down from the pond surface.

Water beetle: A small, shiny beetle that can often be seen whirling around on the pond surface.

Leech: A water worm, the leech spends most of its time resting near or on pond plants or stones.

Water scorpion: A flat insect with a long breathing tube at its bottom end. It catches minibeasts with its curved front legs.

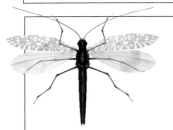

Mayfly: This delicate flying insect rests with its wings closed above its body. It has three hair-like tails at the end of its body.

Caddis fly: A small brown flying insect with long **antennae**.

Pond snail: Pond snails feed on water plants. They belong to the **mollusk** family, like all snails and slugs.

Caddis fly larva: The young of the caddis fly often builds a tube of stones or sticks to protect its body.

Here are some other common minibeasts (remember, there are thousands of different minibeasts—you may need to use a field guide as well):

Great diving beetle larva: One of the biggest larvae in the pond, this is the young of the great diving beetle. It swims about catching whatever it can to eat, including small fish.

Bee: Bees are flying insects and there are many different types. Some collect mud from the pond's edge.

Dragonfly nymph: The young of the dragonfly, this nymph has six legs and big eyes, like the adult.

Beetle: There are thousands of types of beetle. Beetles are insects and they have two pairs of wings. One set is hard to protect the soft set underneath.

Damselfly nymph: The young of the damselfly, this nymph has three feather-like tails at its bottom end.

Freshwater shrimp: A small pale animal that is a **crustacean**, like the shrimps people eat.

Mayfly nymph: Smaller than the dragonfly and damselfly nymphs, the young of the mayfly has three long, slim "tails."

Water flea: A tiny see-through animal that lives in water.

Glossary

Algae Tiny plants that live in water.

Animals A huge group of living things including birds, insects, mammals, mollusks, reptiles and amphibians.

Antennae Feelers on an insect's head and used for smell, taste, and touch.

Backbone The line of bones down the middle of the skeleton.

Bug The name for an insect with piercing mouth parts, used to suck sap from a plant or blood from another animal.

Compound eyes Each insect eye is made up of many tiny lenses joined together in one eye. This allows insects to see all around them.

Crustacean A large group of animals whose skeletons are on the outside, including crabs, shrimp, and lobsters.

Food chain A food chain shows how living things are linked by what they eat.

Habitat A place where certain plants and animals like to live. Habitats can be small, like a pond, or huge, like an ocean.

Insects A huge group of animals. All insects have a body in three parts—the head at one end, the thorax in the middle, and the abdomen at the other end. Six legs are attached to the thorax, and many insects also have wings.

Invertebrates A huge group of animals that don't have a backbone, including insects, worms, and spiders.

Larva (*plural,* larvae) The stage in the lifecycle of many insects after they hatch from eggs.

Lens The part of the eye that focuses light.

Life cycle The lifetime of a living thing from birth until death. An insect life cycle often goes through these stages: egg, larva (nymph), pupa, and adult.

Mollusks A group of animals that has a soft body, including the snail, slug, and octopus.

Nymph A type of larva (see left).

Predator An animal that eats other animals, instead of plants.

Prey Animals that other animals hunt to eat.

Pupa (*plural,* pupae) The part of the life cycle of many insects before they turn into adults.

Tadpole The young of a frog or toad.

Wingspan The width of an insect across its wings when they are fully spread out.

Web Sites to Visit

http://www.rspb.org/wildlife/wildlifegarden/
An informative web site with an A-Z guide to many minibeasts that you could find in a garden or pond.

www.naturegrid.org.uk/pondexplorer/ pondexplorer.html
A great web site where you can do a virtual pond dip—ideal if you don't have a pond nearby. There is also lots of other information about the pond habitat.

Note to Parents and Teachers:
Every effort has been made by the publishers to ensure that these web sites are suitable for children, that they are of the highest educational value, and that they contain no inappropriate or offensive material. However, because of the nature of the Internet, it is impossible to guarantee that the contents of these sites will not be altered. We strongly advise that Internet access is supervised by a responsible adult.

Index